mix & match tracing books

·SPACE·

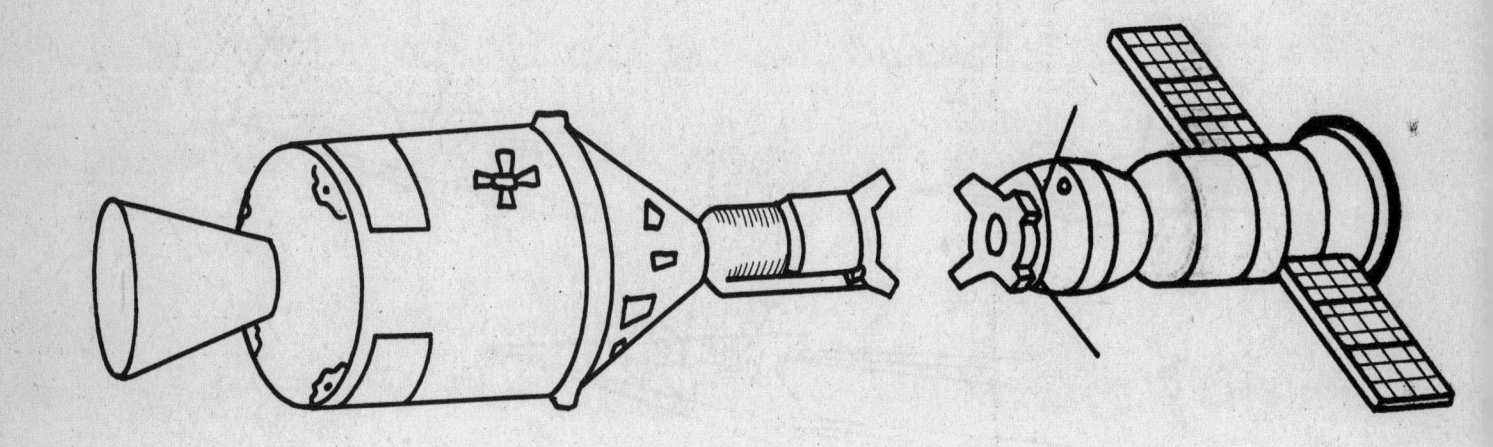

By Mary Damon

Copyright ©1988 by RGA Publishing Group, Inc.
Copyright ©1988 cover illustration by Lesley Boney
Published by Price Stern Sloan, Inc.
360 North La Cienega Blvd., Los Angeles, CA 90048

Printed in the United States of America. All rights reserved. No part of this publication may be reproduced, stored in a retrieval system or transmitted, in any form or by any means, electronic, mechanical photocopying, recording or otherwise, without the prior written permission of the publishers.
ISBN: 0-8431-2247-1

10 9 8 7 6 5 4 3 2

PRICE STERN SLOAN

Los Angeles

Mix & Match Tracing Books
SPACE

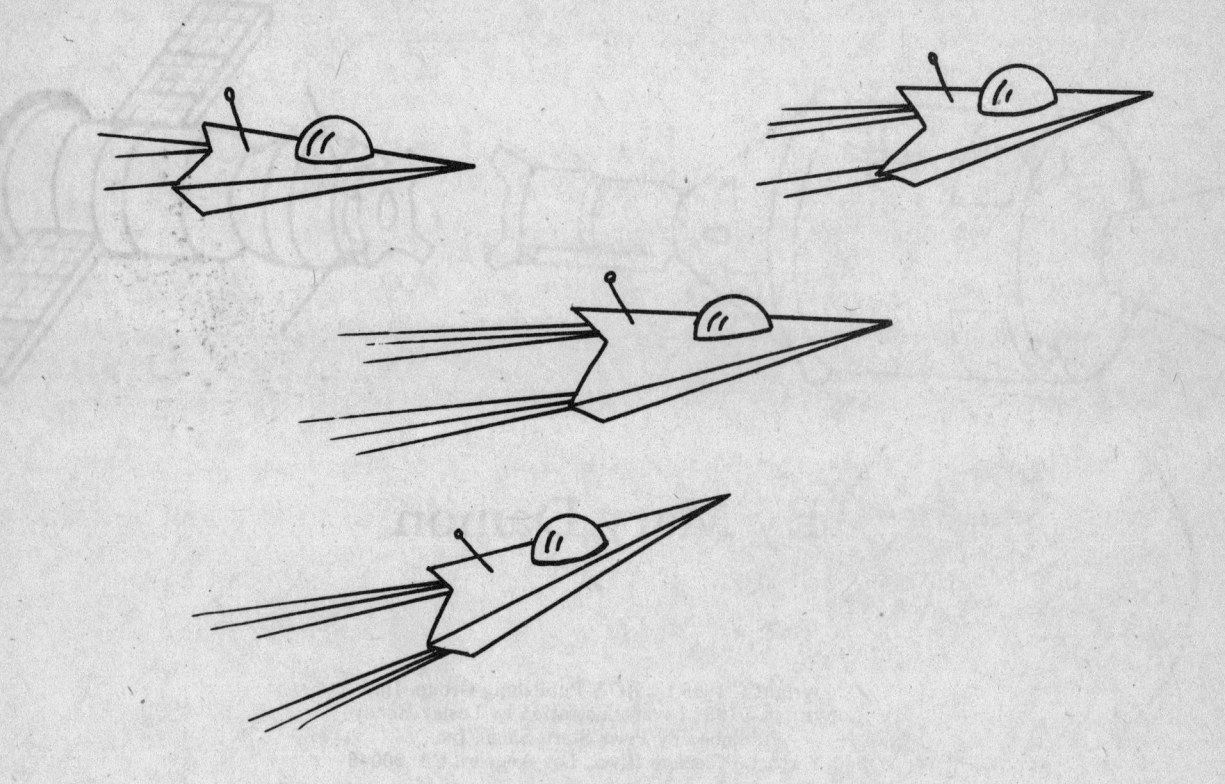

Planets

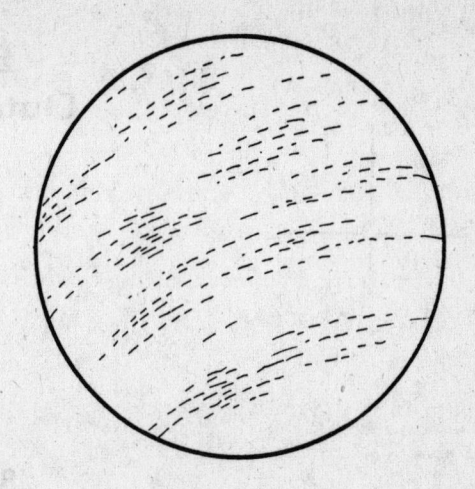

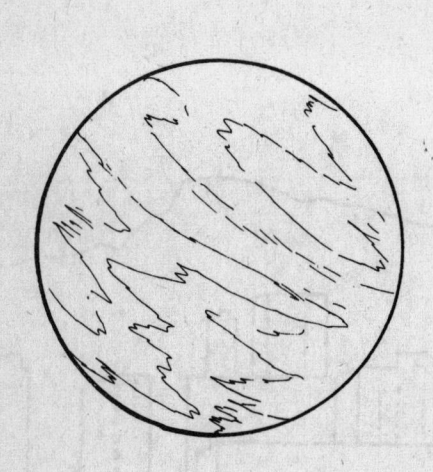

**Earth
Outer Space**

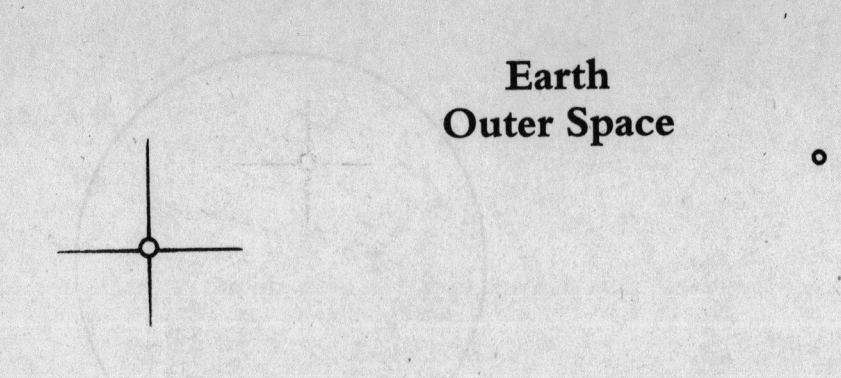

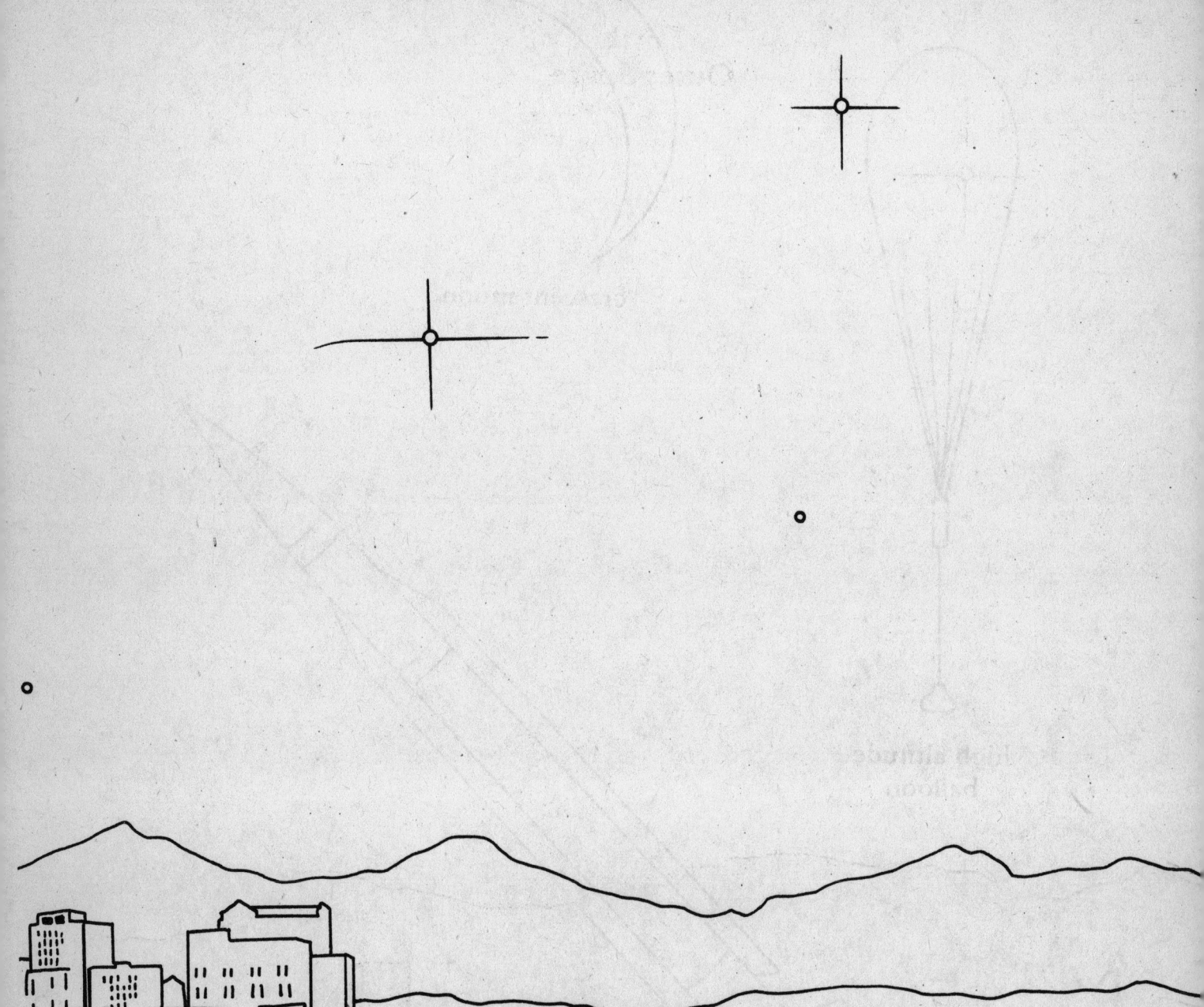

Earth

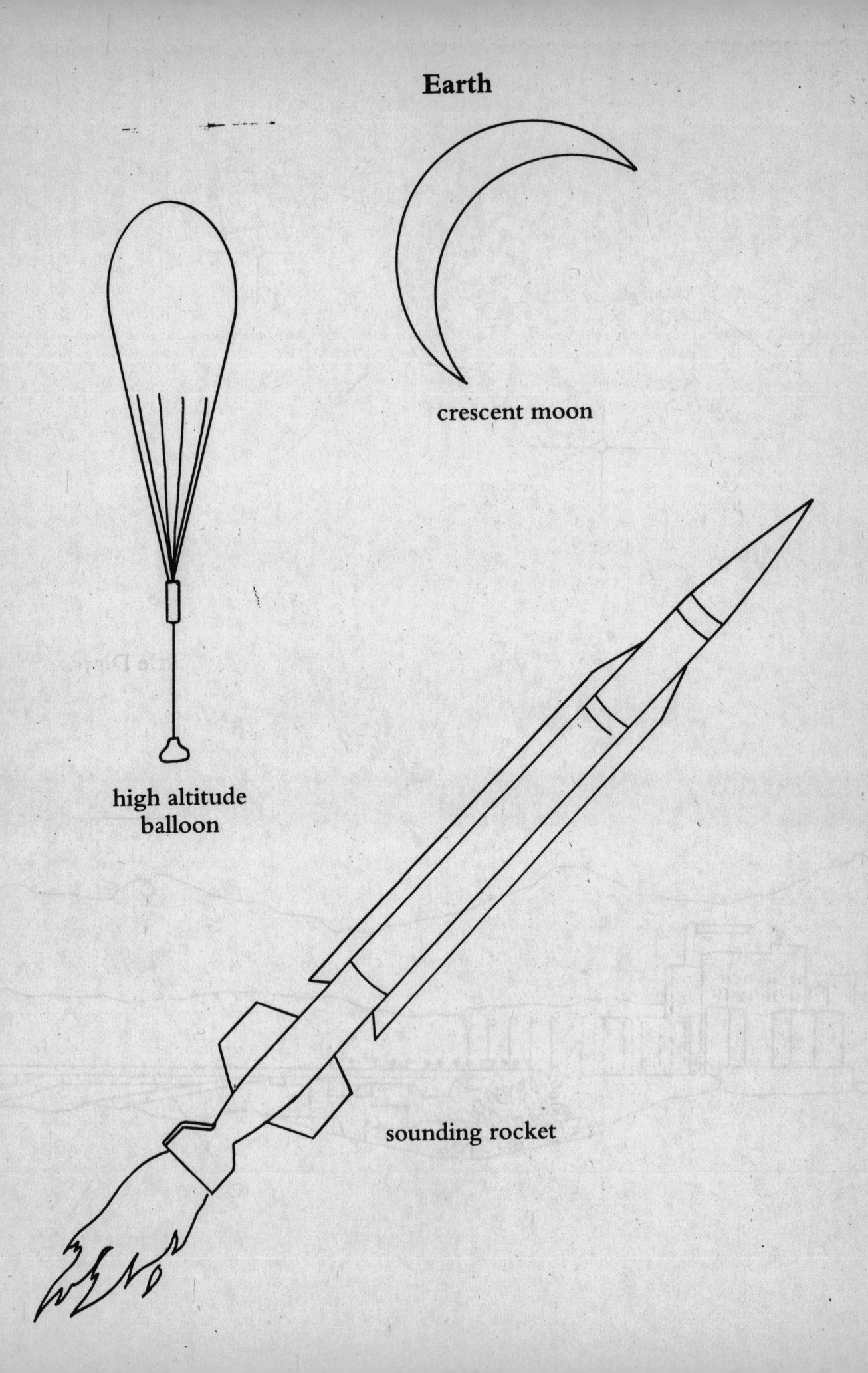

crescent moon

high altitude
balloon

sounding rocket

Constellations

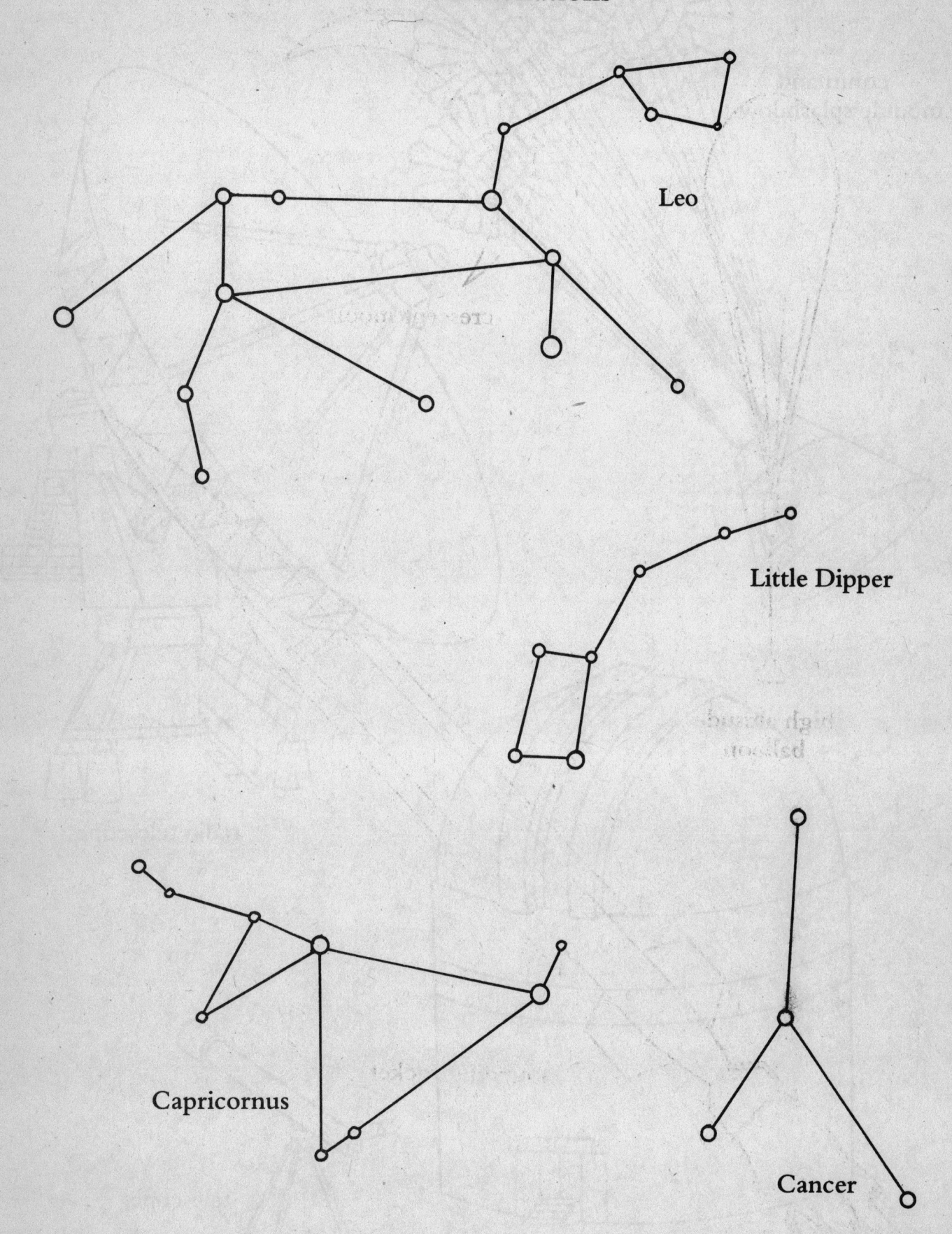

Leo

Little Dipper

Capricornus

Cancer

command module splashdown

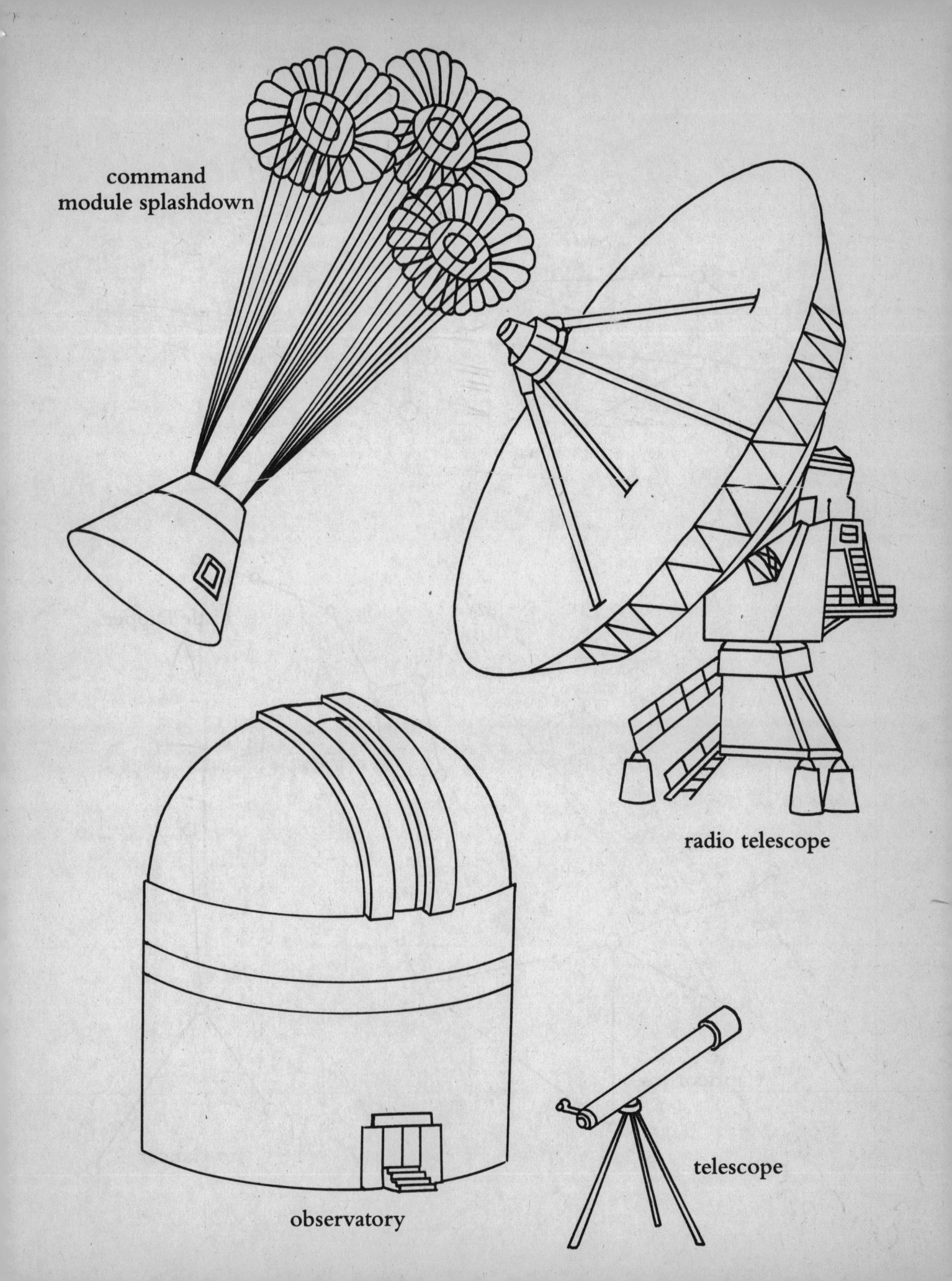

radio telescope

observatory

telescope

Space Exploration

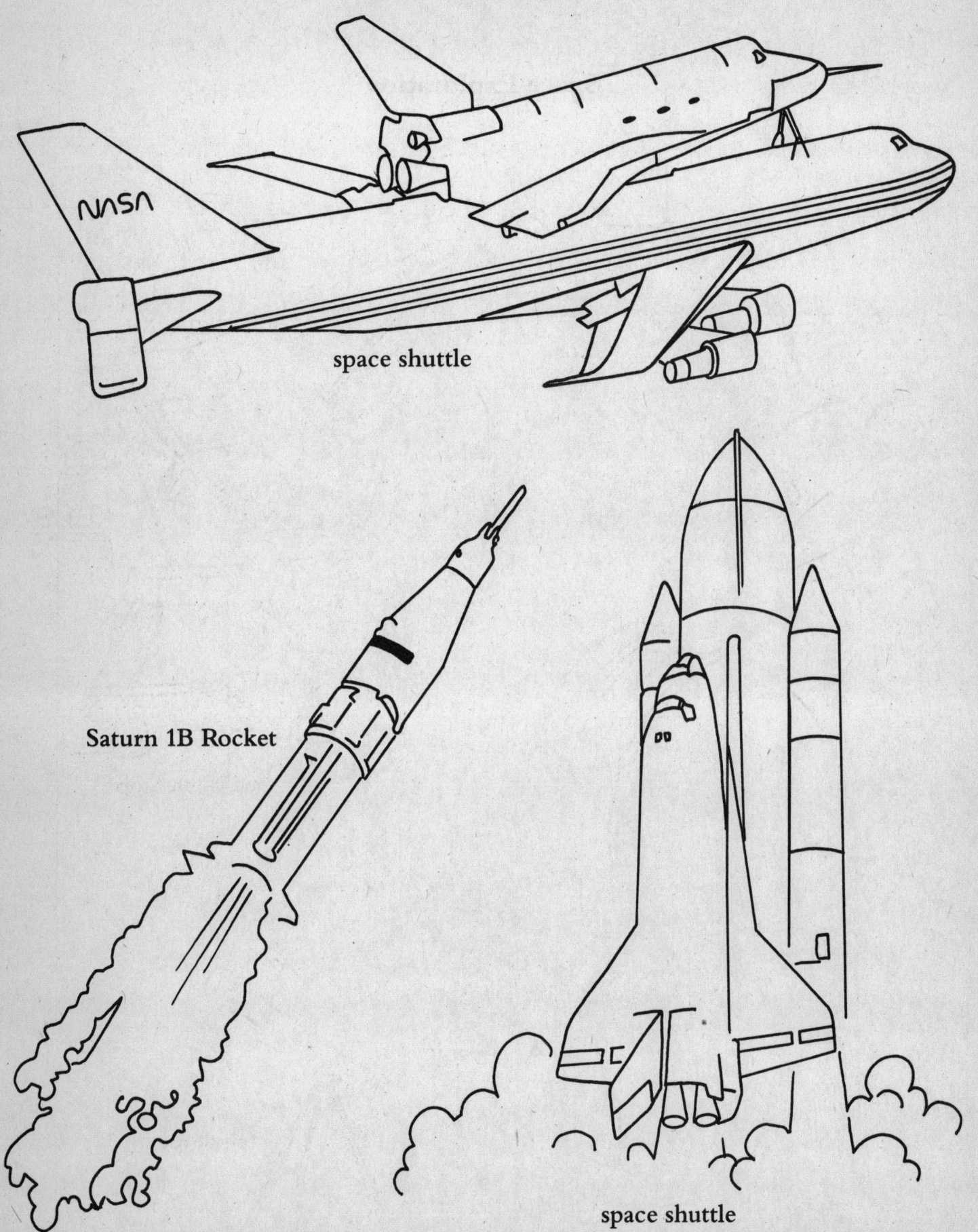

space shuttle

Saturn 1B Rocket

space shuttle

> # Space Exploration

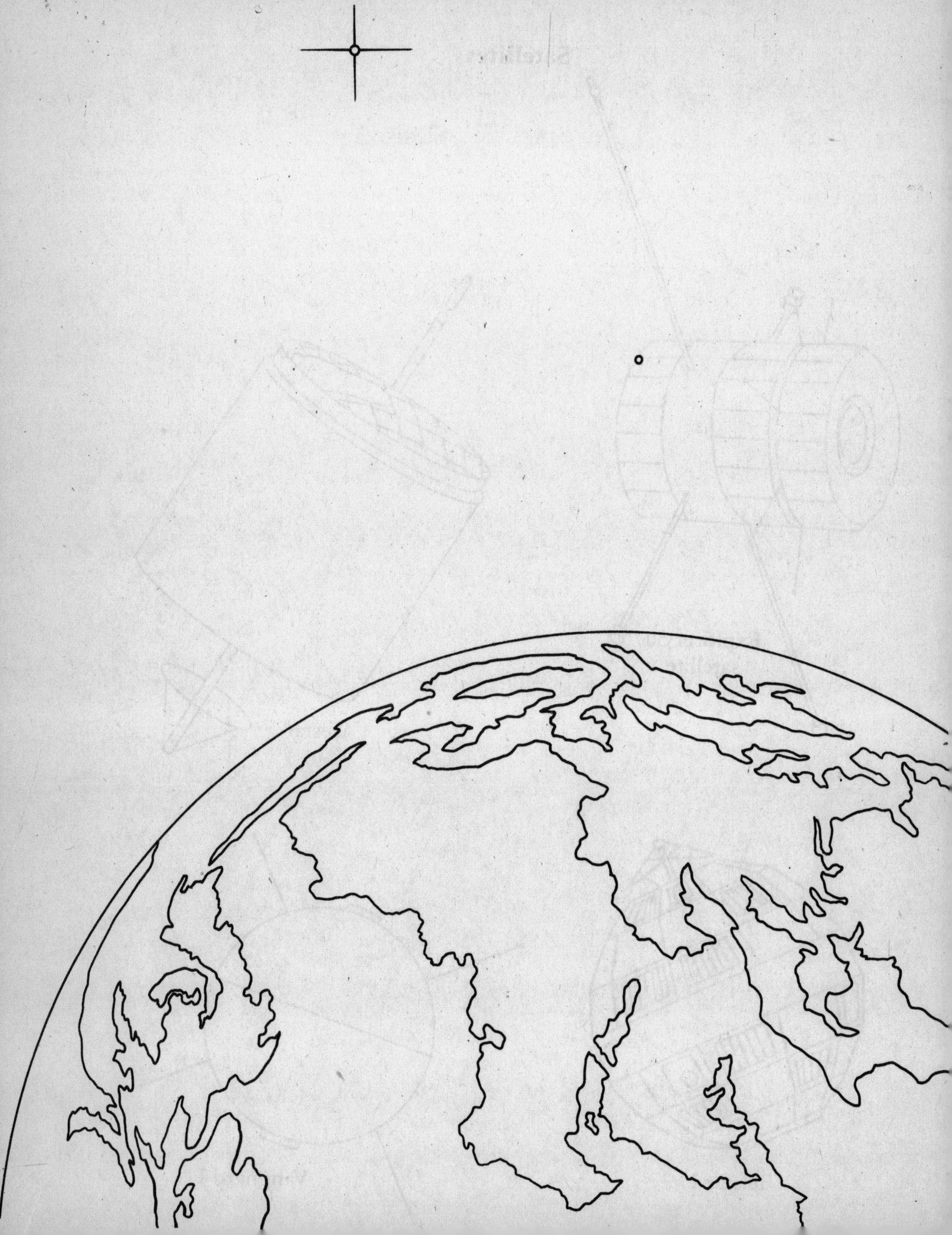

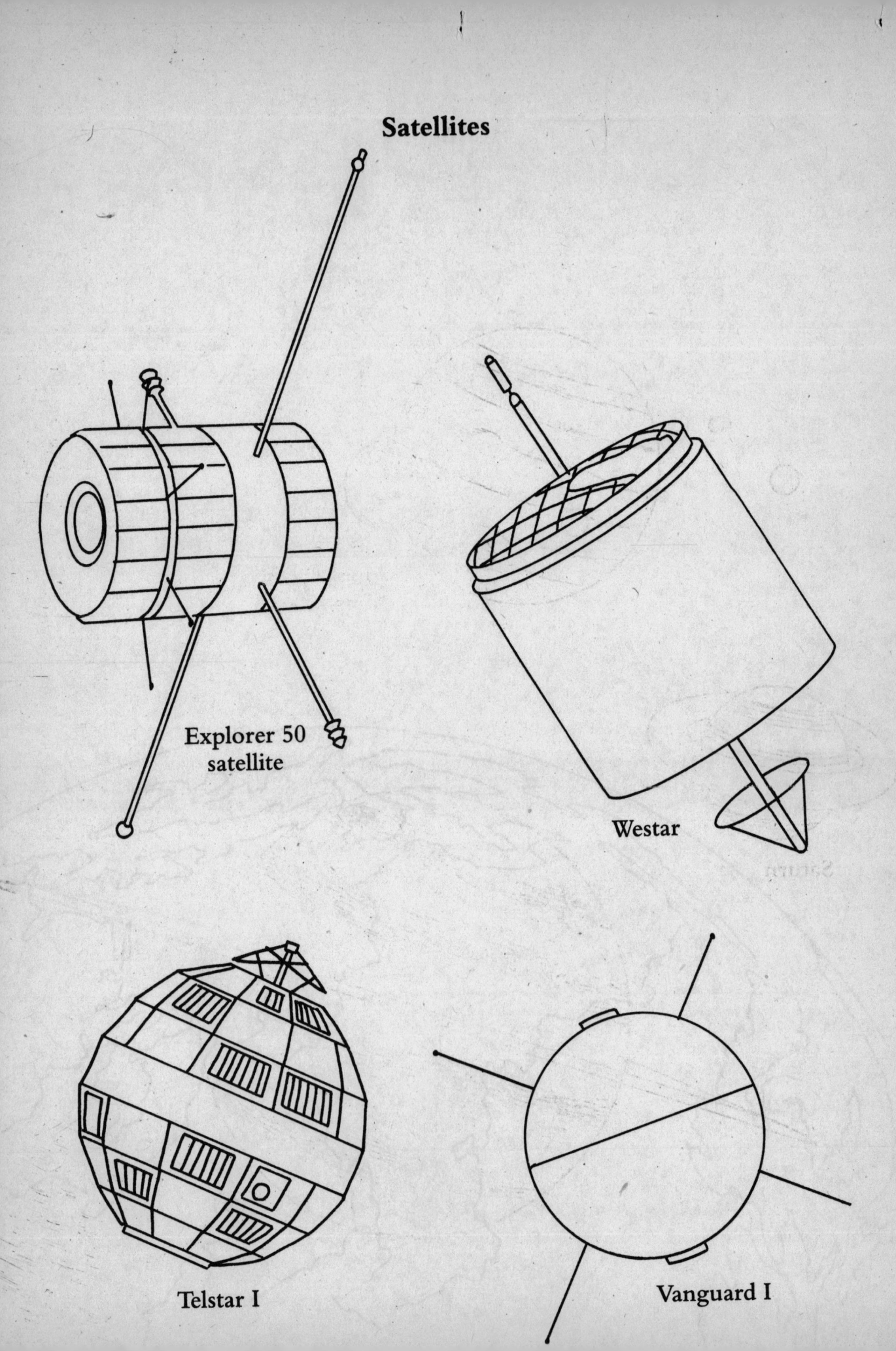

Satellites

Explorer 50 satellite

Westar

Telstar I

Vanguard I

Planets

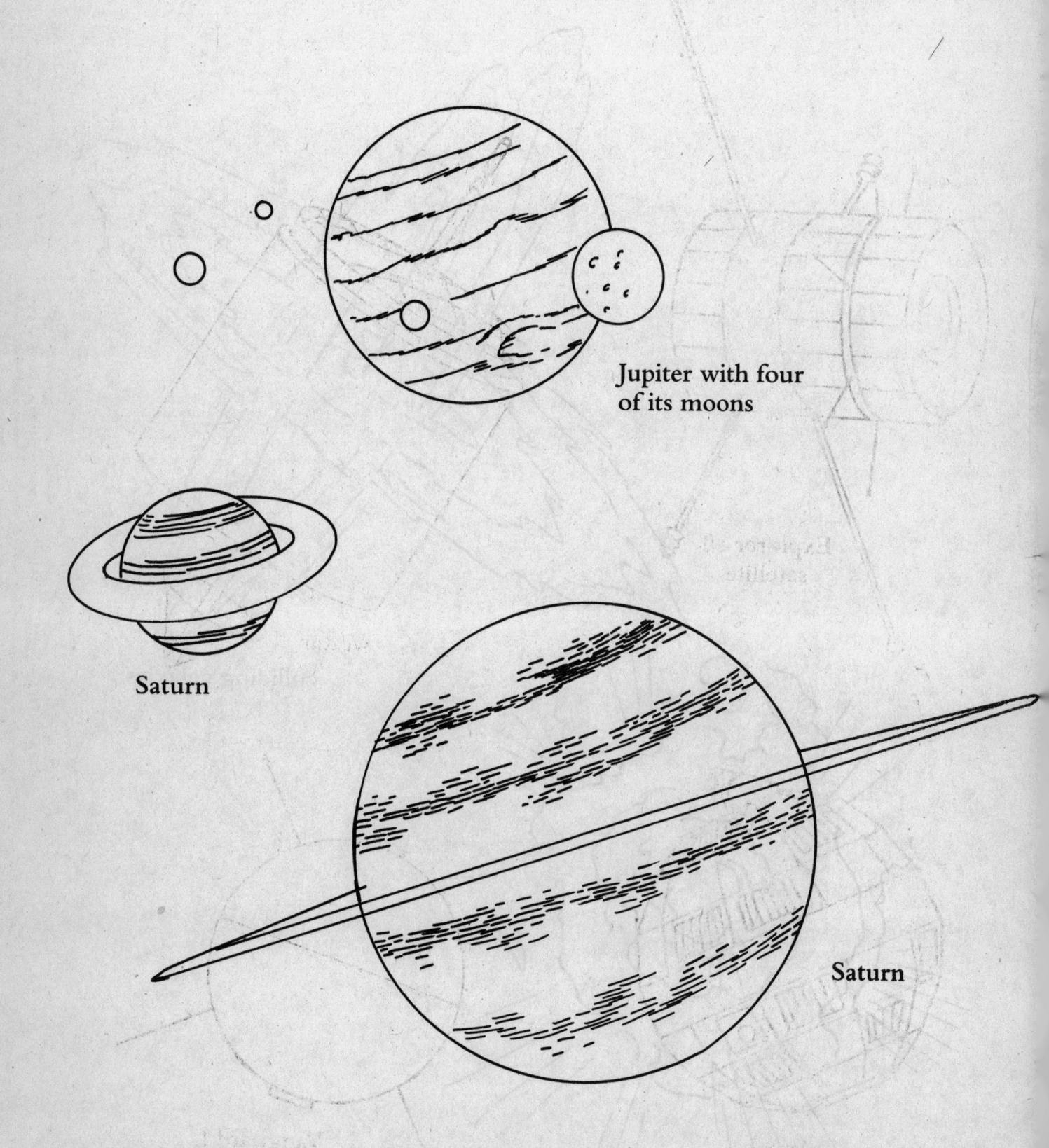

Jupiter with four of its moons

Saturn

Saturn

Space Phenomena

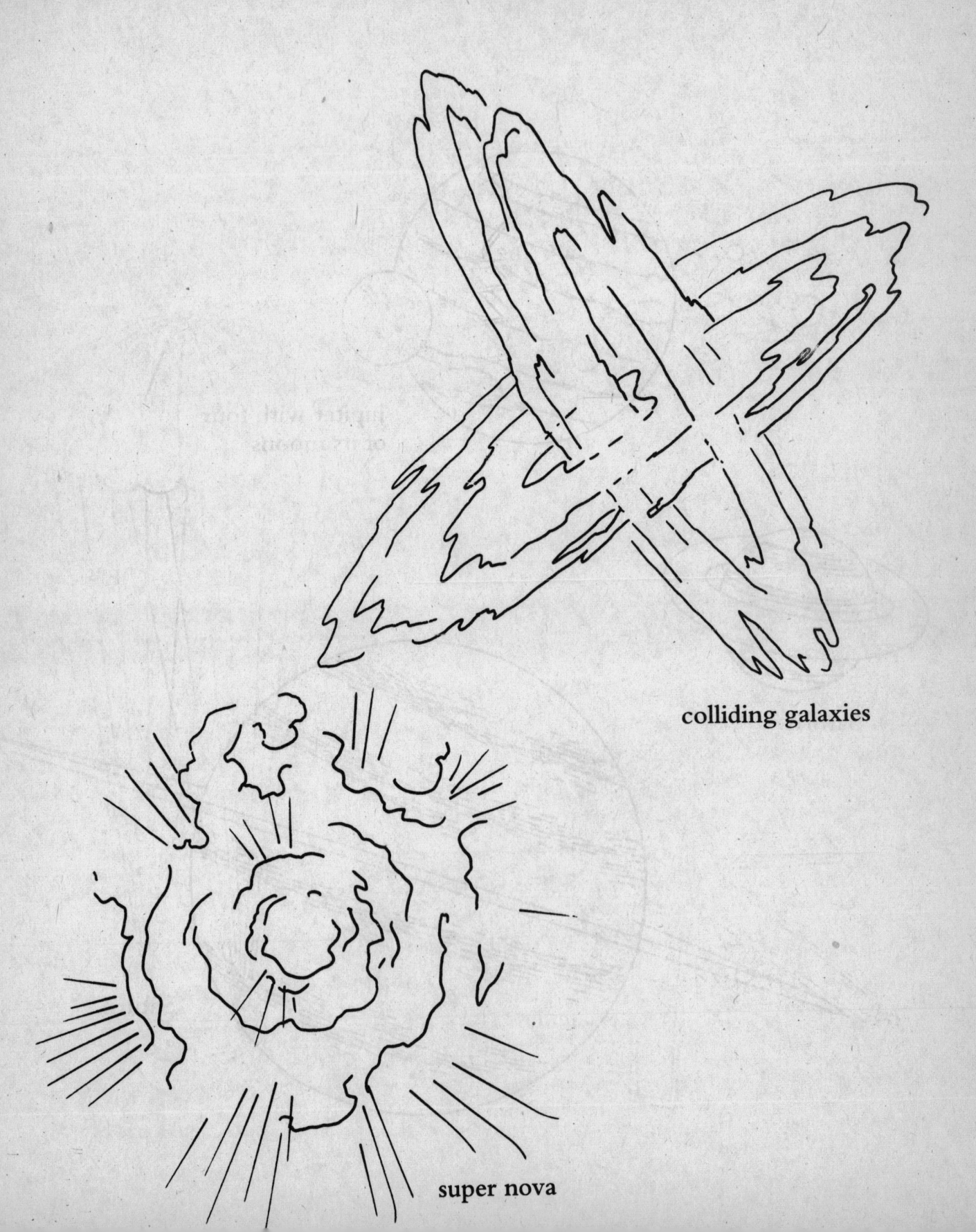

colliding galaxies

super nova

Satellites

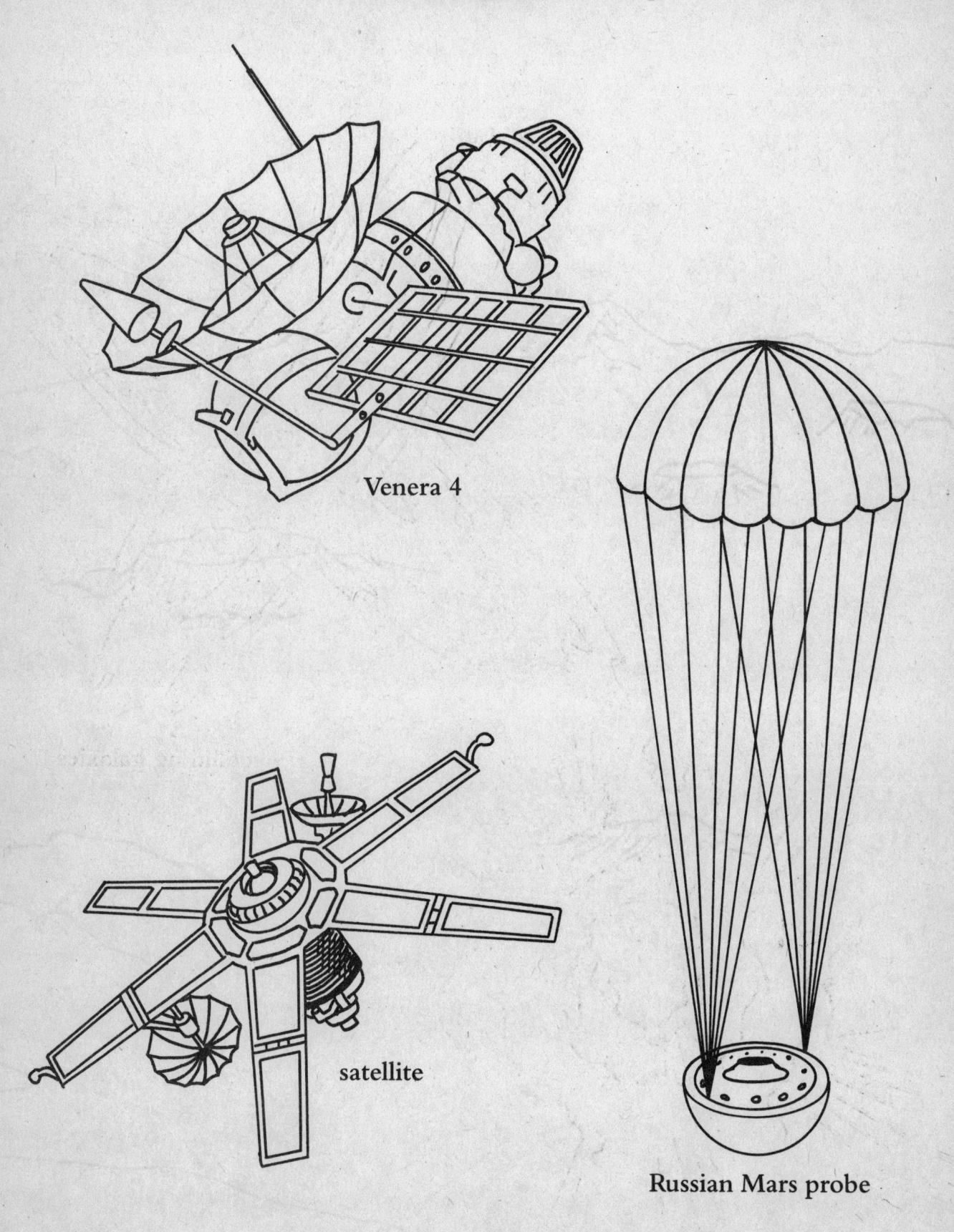

Venera 4

satellite

Russian Mars probe

Moonscape

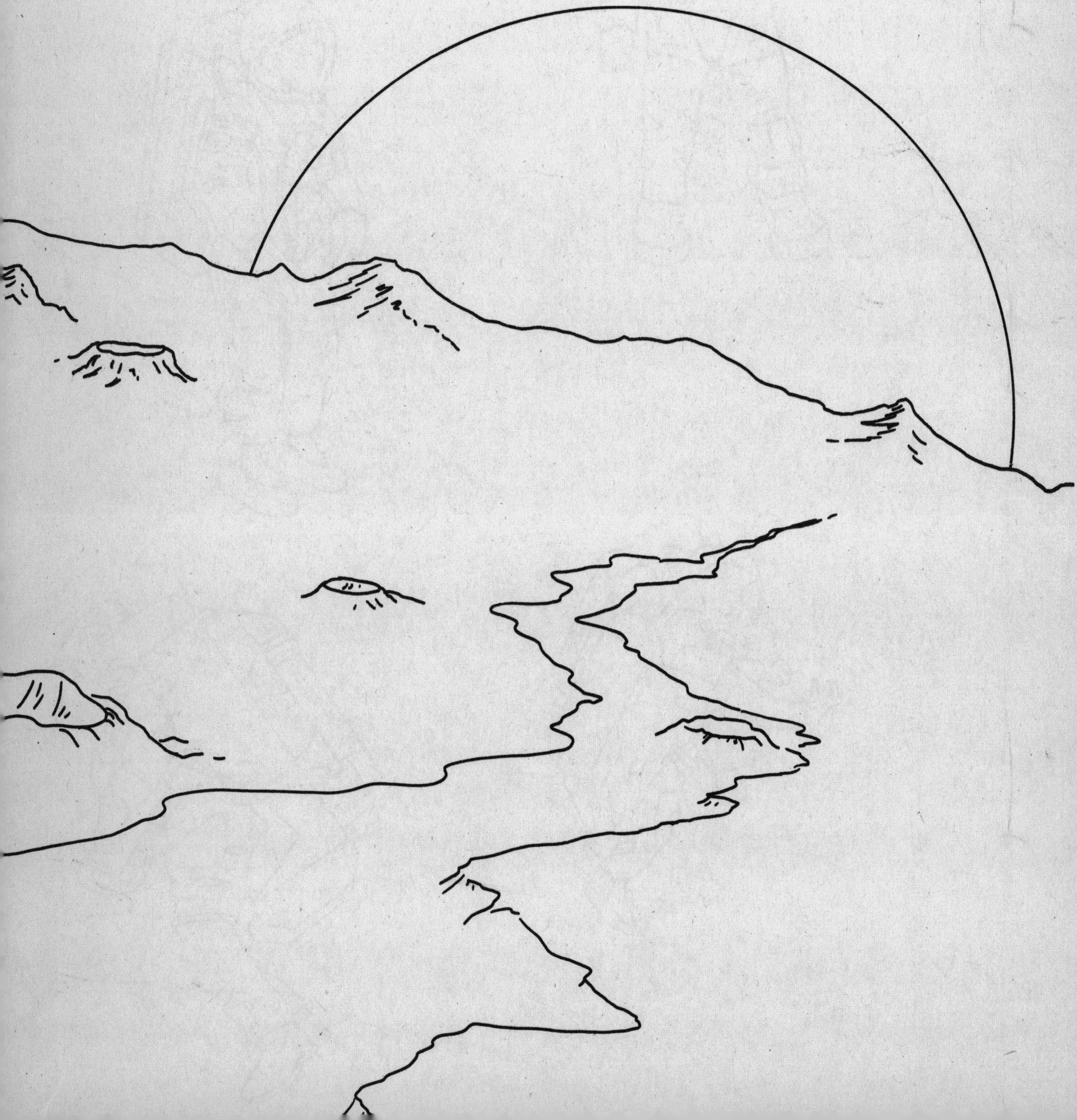

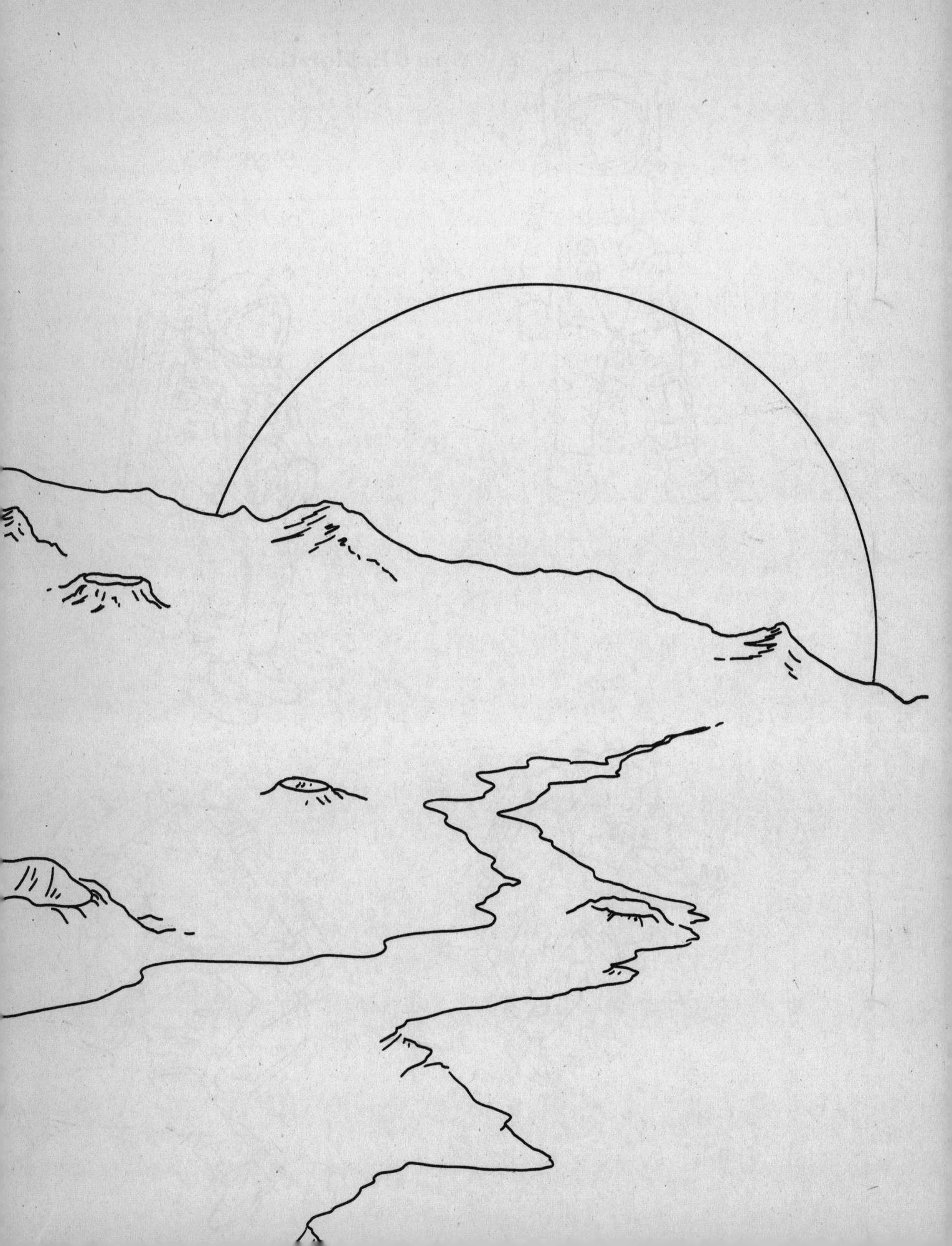

Space Exploration

astronauts

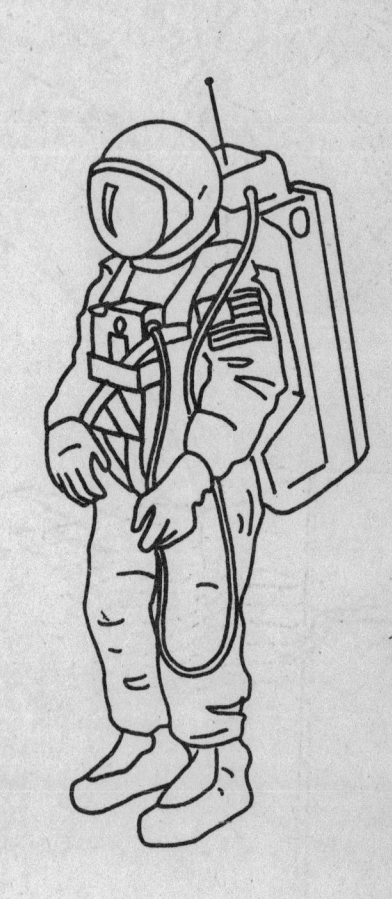

Gemini VII

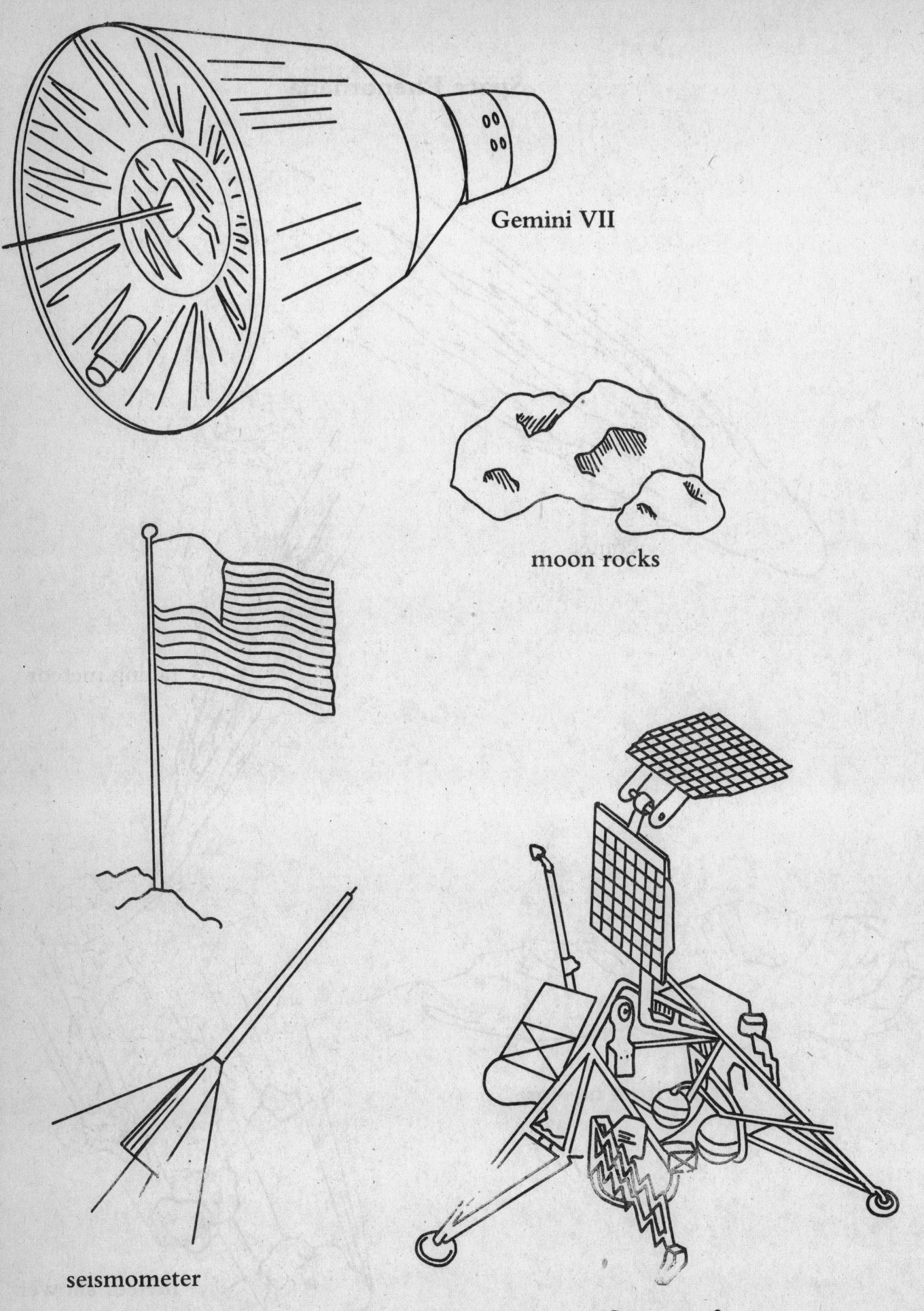

moon rocks

seismometer

Surveyor 3

Space Phenomena

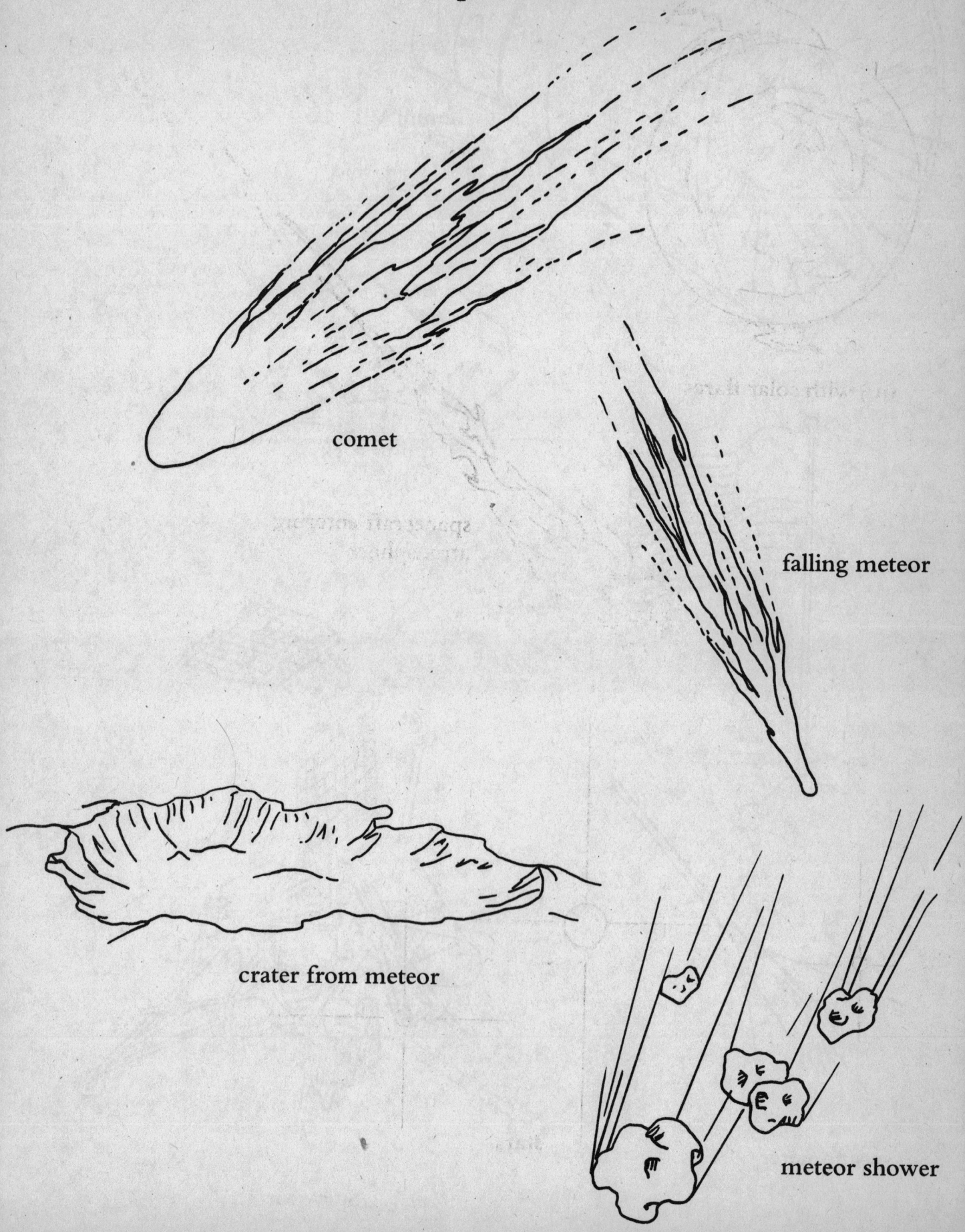

comet

falling meteor

crater from meteor

meteor shower

sun with solar flares

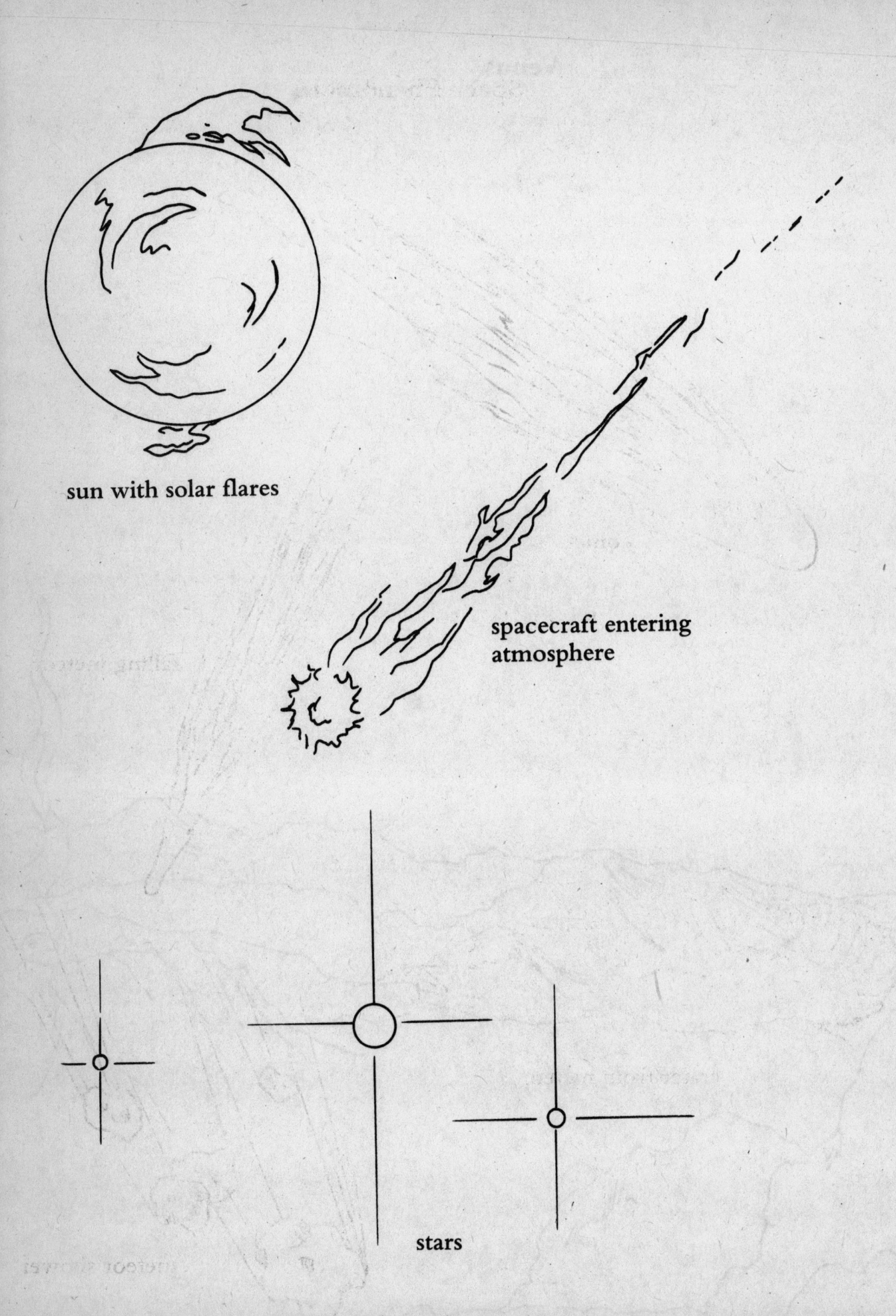

spacecraft entering atmosphere

stars

Venus

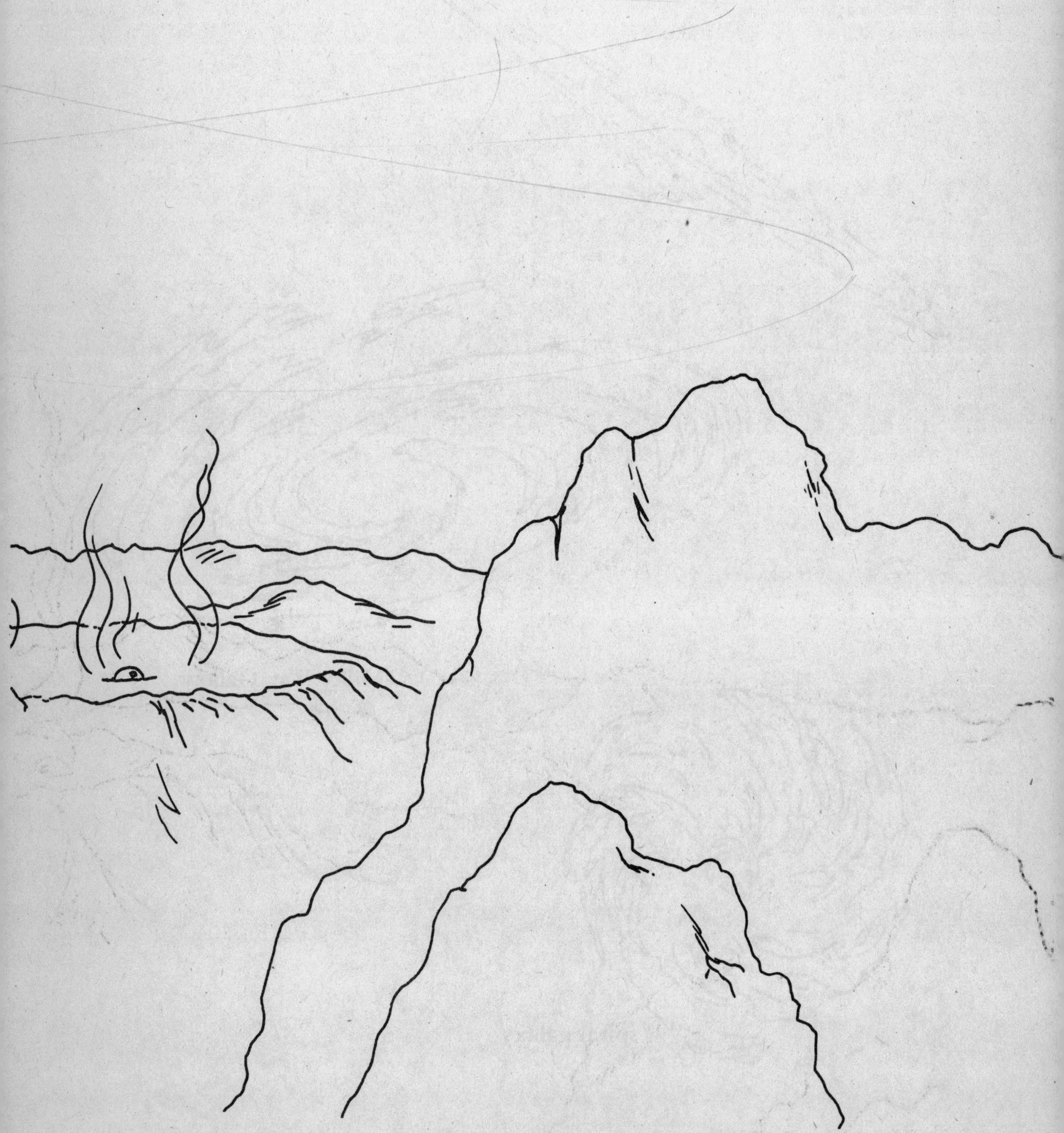

Galaxies

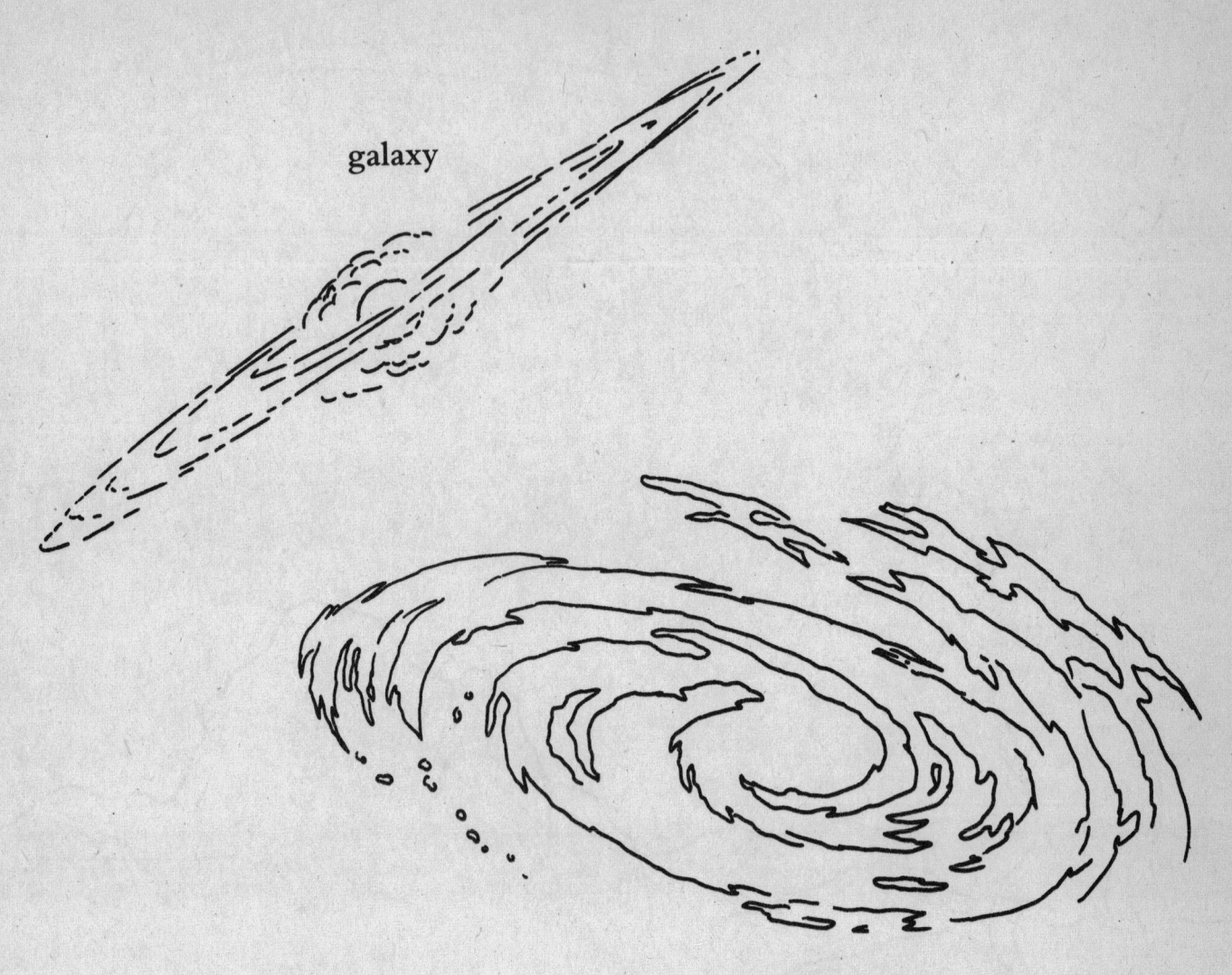

galaxy

Milky Way Galaxy

spiral galaxy

Space Flight

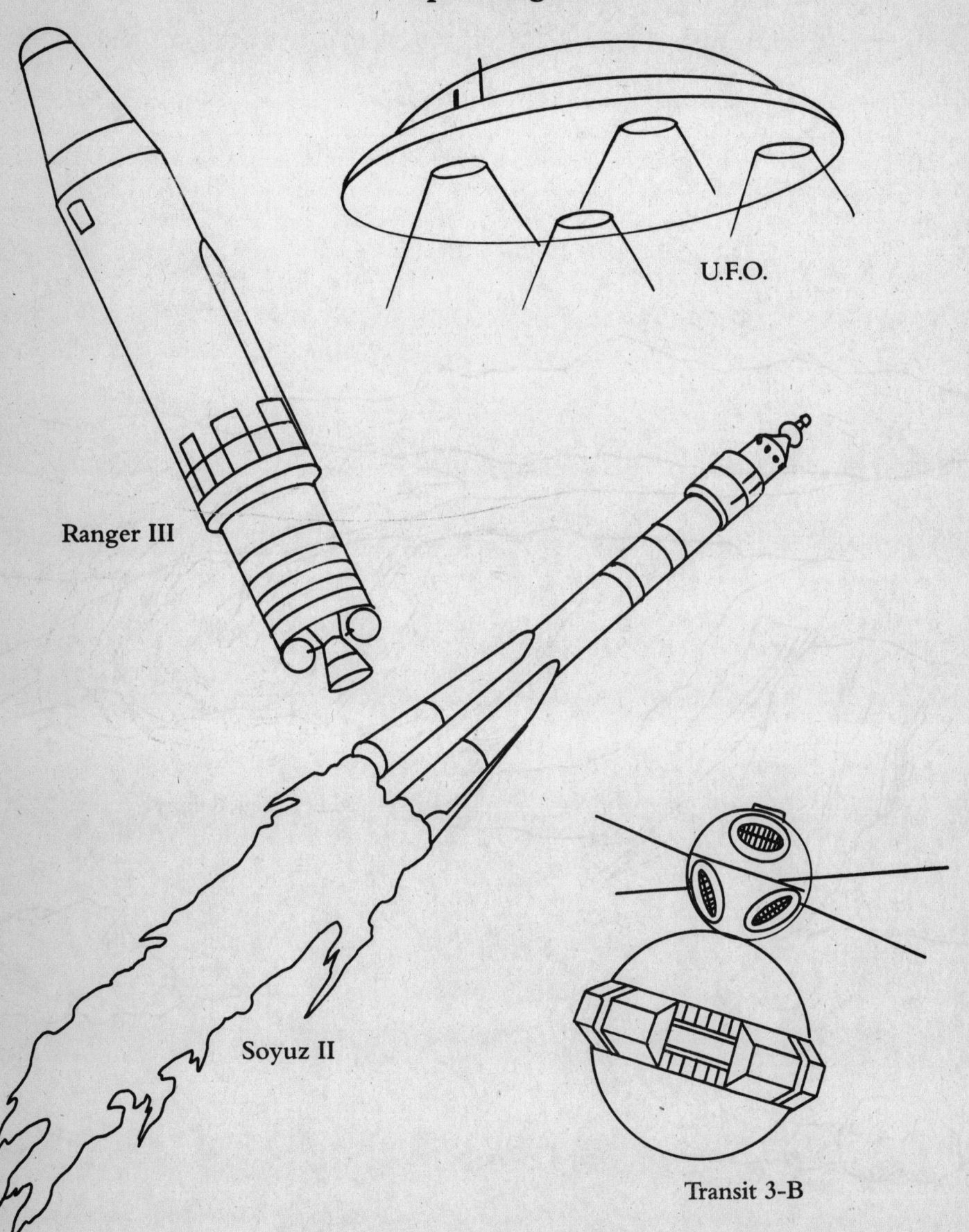

Ranger III

U.F.O.

Soyuz II

Transit 3-B

Mars

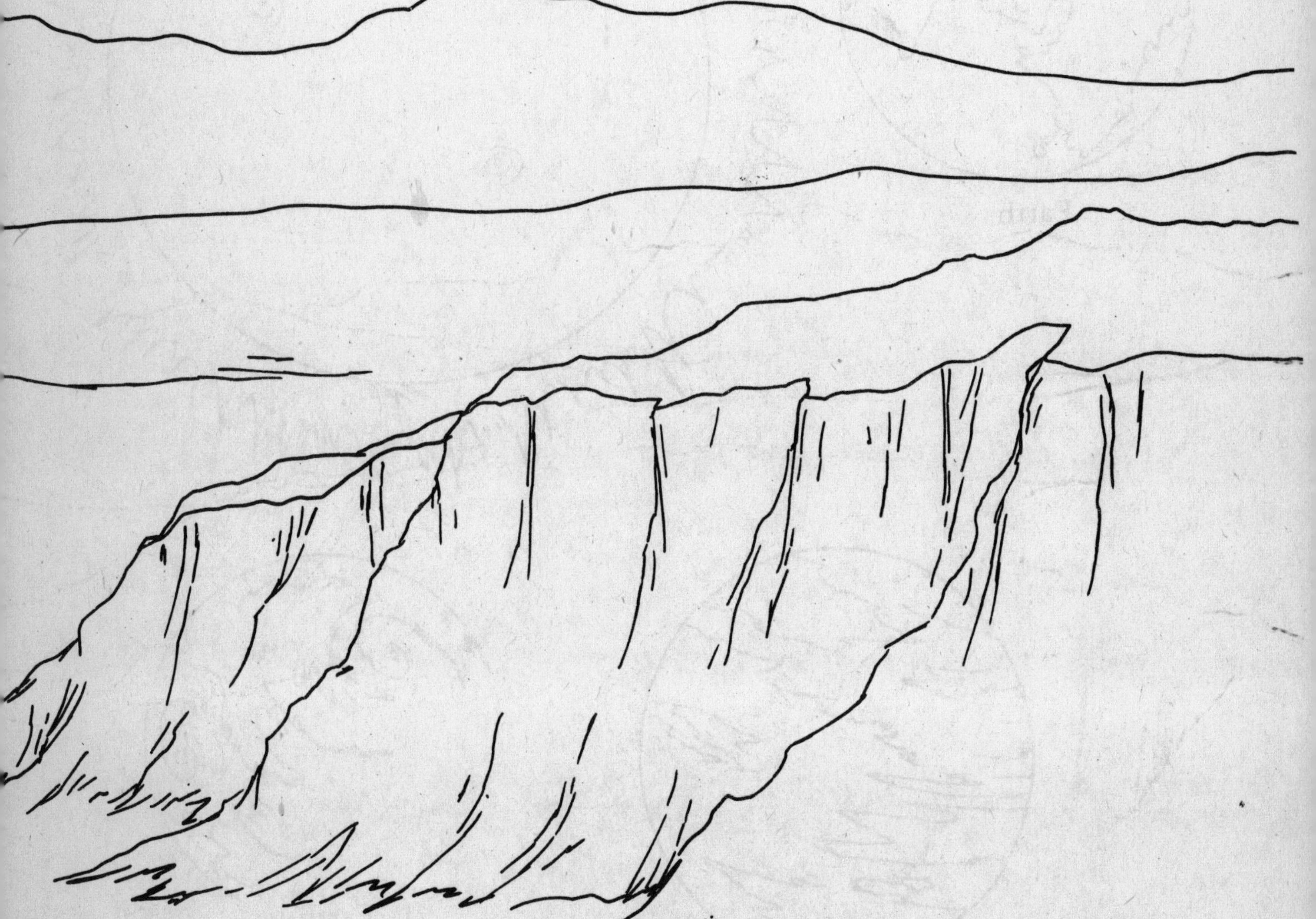

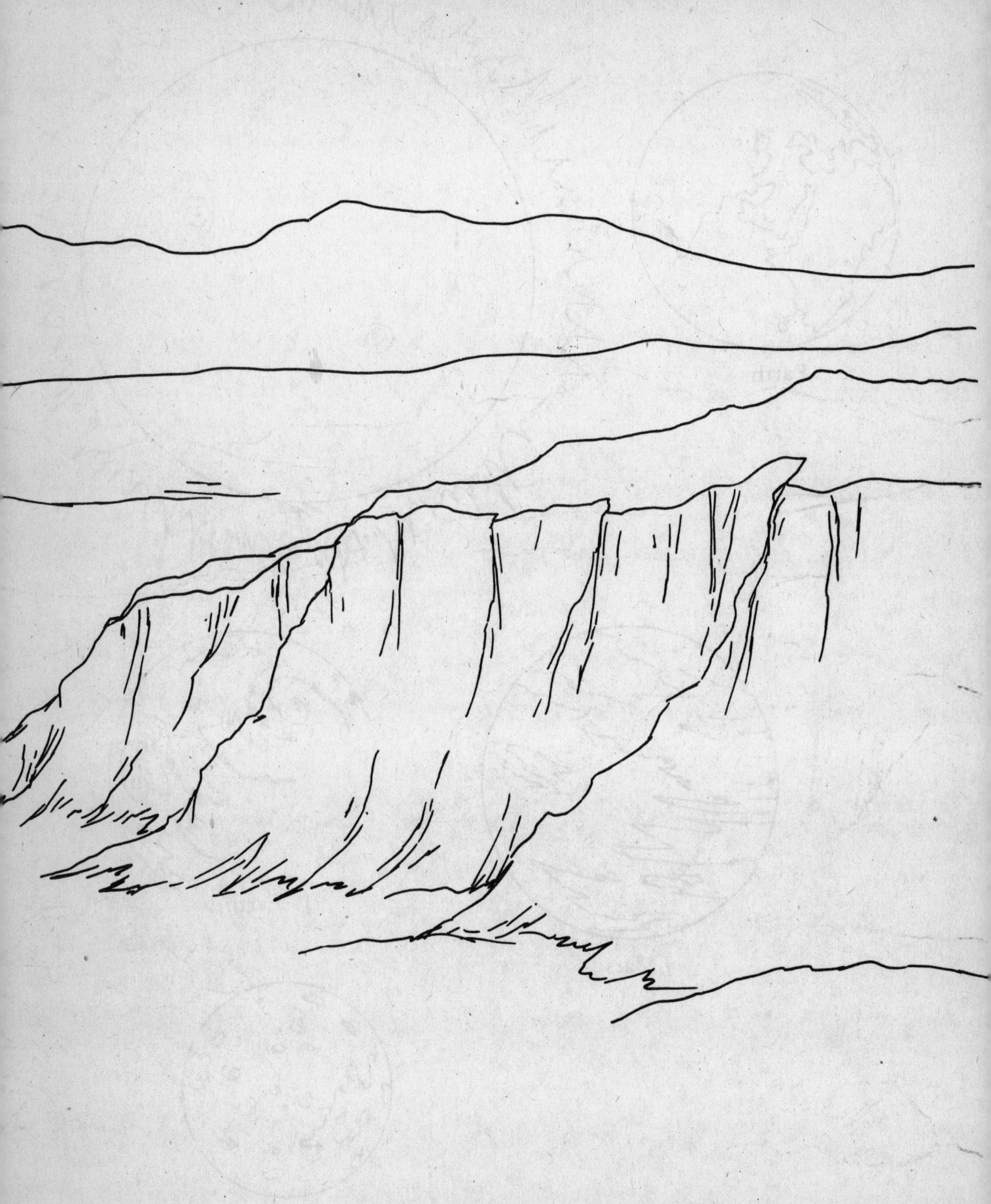

Earth

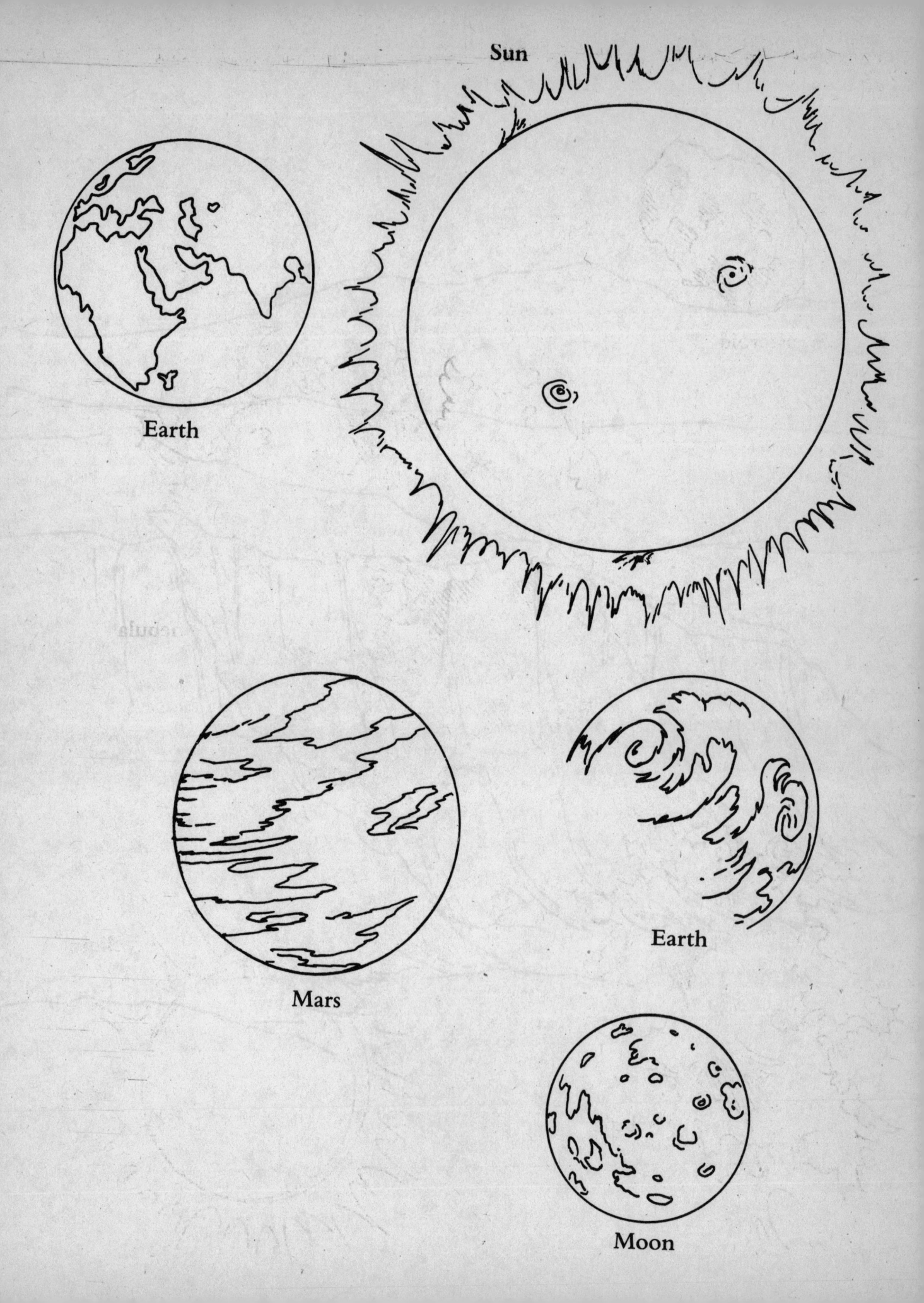

Sun

Mars

Earth

Moon

In our solar system

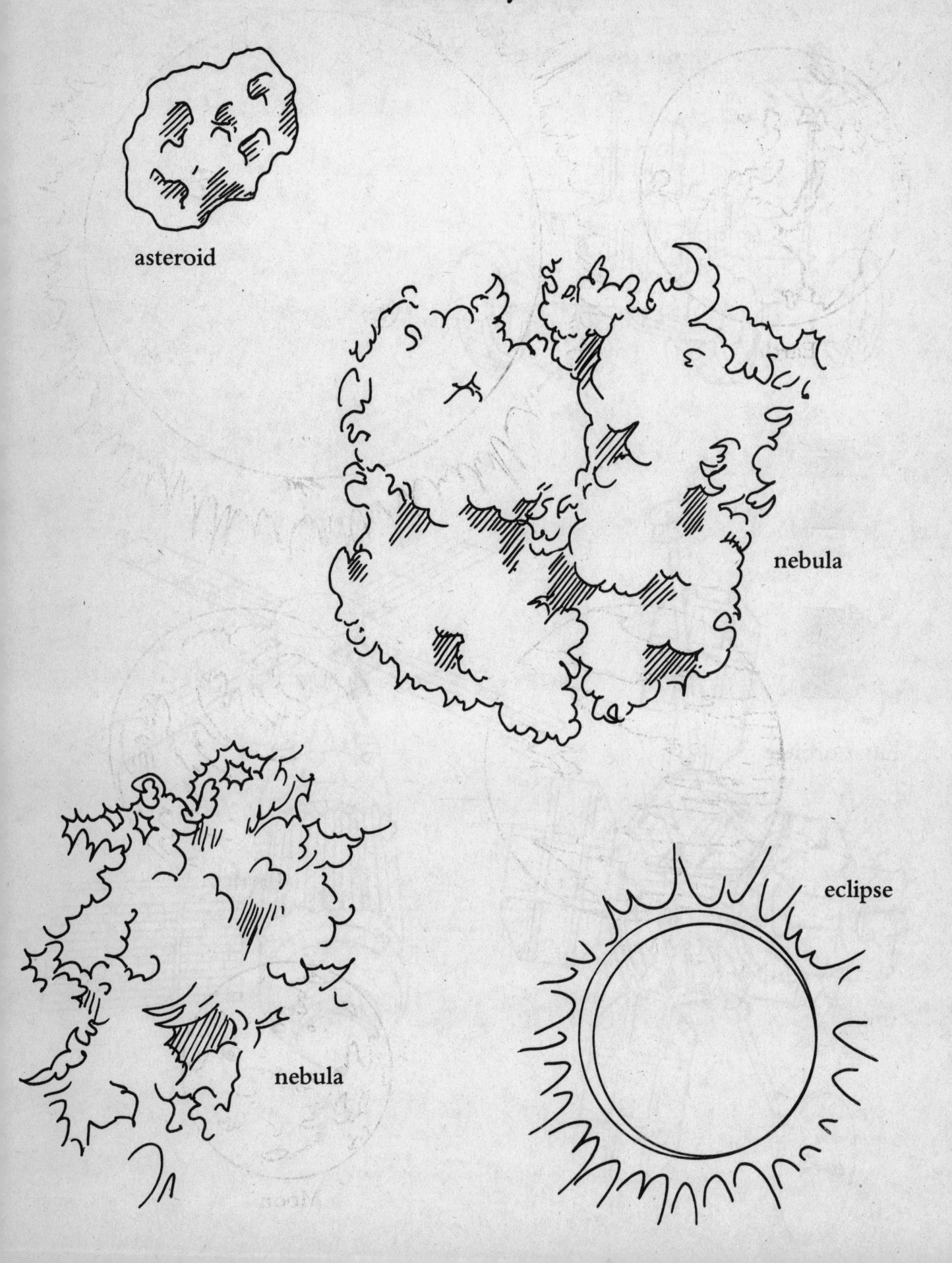

asteroid

nebula

nebula

eclipse

Space Exploration

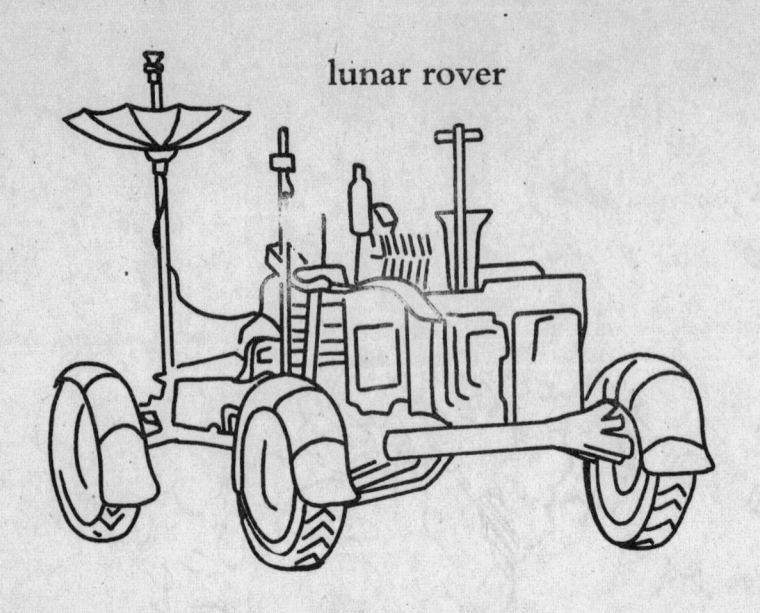

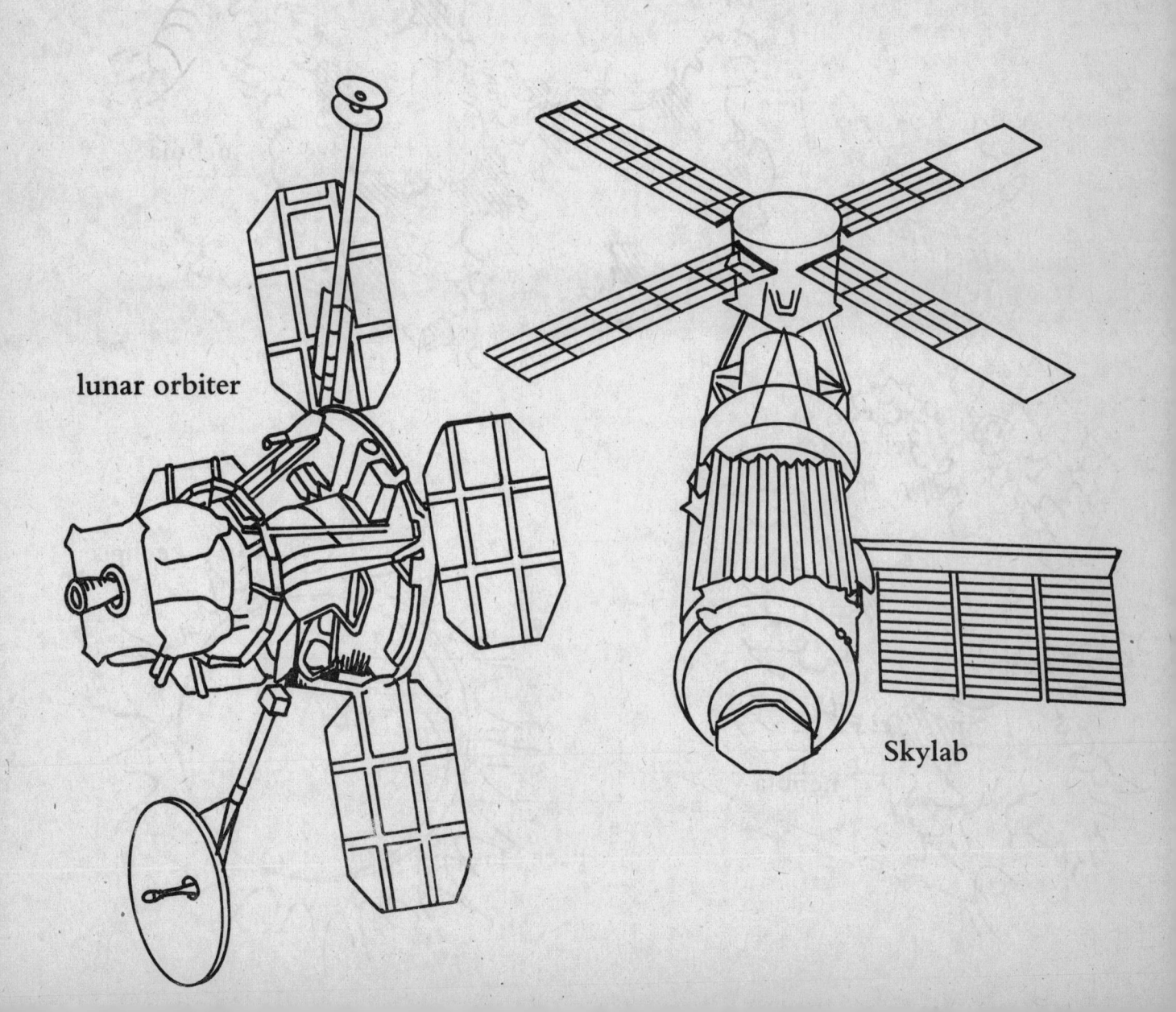

lunar rover

lunar orbiter

Skylab

footprints

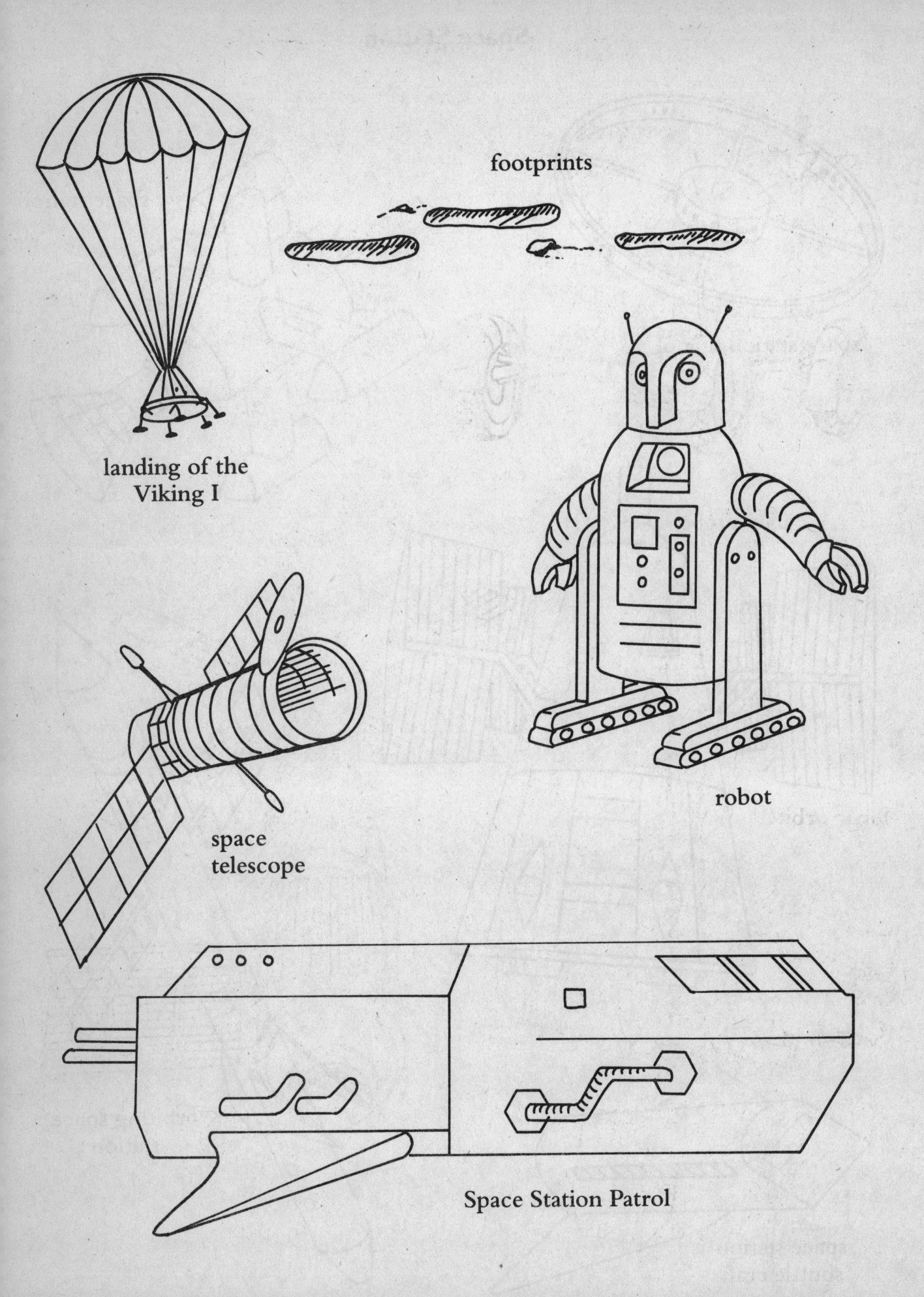

landing of the
Viking I

space
telescope

robot

Space Station Patrol

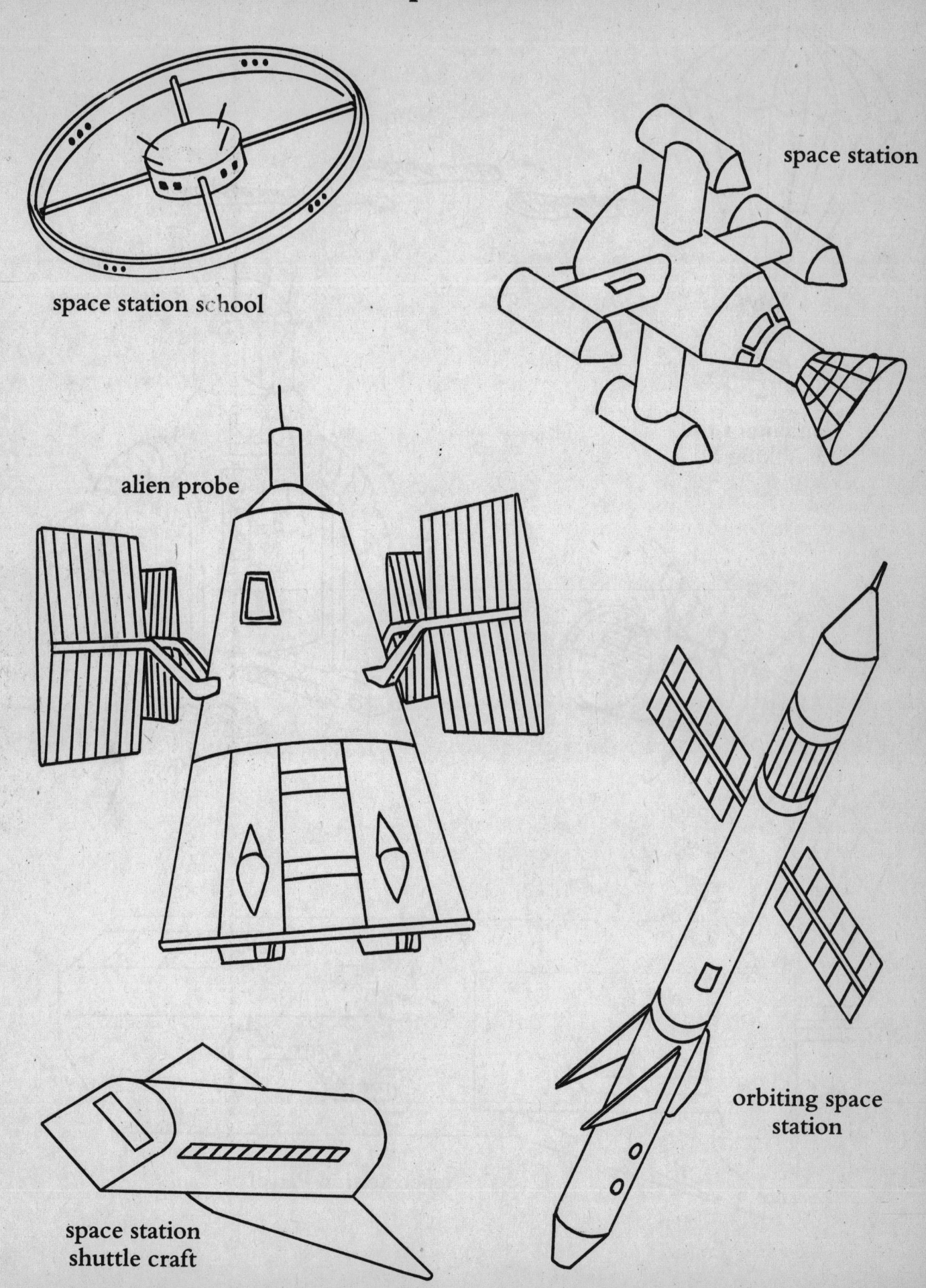

Space Station

space station school

space station

alien probe

space station shuttle craft

orbiting space station